# Quit

S

9   8
Digit on the right indicates the number of this printing
Library of Congress Cataloging-in-Publication Number
2001087032
ISBN 0-7624-1070-1

Edited by Nancy Armstrong
Typography: Times & Kabel

This book may be ordered by mail from the publisher.
Please include $2.50 for postage and handling.
*But try your bookstore first!*

Running Press Book Publishers
125 South Twenty-second Street
Philadelphia, Pennsylvania 19103-4399
**Visit us on the web!**
**www.runningpress.com**

## Books by Charles F. Wetherall

Quit: Read This Book and Stop Smoking

Quit II: A Woman's Guide to Stop Smoking

How to Get Someone You Love
to Quit Smoking

Quit for Teens

Passport Weight Loss

Weight Loss through Willpower

Winter Weight Loss and Fitness Guide

Exercising Personal Excellence

How to Get Yourself to Stay on Any Diet

Diet: Read This Book and Stay Slim Forever

Kicking the Coffee Habit

The Gifted Kids Guide to Puzzles and
Mind Games

The Gifted Kids Guide to Creativity

*To the 50,000,000 people
in the United States who
want to quit smoking:
this pocket-sized book
can make it
possible.*

# CONTENTS

# Before You Quit

The more things change, the more they remain the same.

More than twenty years have slipped by since this book was first written. And although it has been rewritten and updated several times, much has changed since its beginning. But far too much has not.

In 1979, the Internet and desktop computers were in their infancy. A loaf of bread cost little more than a quarter. Cigarettes were about 60¢ a pack. Some 300,000 Americans died that year from smoking and fifty million men and women continued to smoke.

Since then, Microsoft founder Bill Gates has become a multi-billionaire riding the worldwide computer phenomena. The price of that loaf of bread has soared at least sixfold. Cigarettes have hit $3 a pack. Some 500,000 now die each year from smoking.

And fifty million men and women still continue to smoke, even in light of several significant new developments that have made quitting easier. This newly-revised work for the new millennium makes note of two of these: the World Wide Web, a bountiful source of quit-smoking information, products, and chat room support; and the various nicotine replacement therapies. Both are making significant contributions to the war on smoking.

But the most important news of the intervening decades is this: since this little book was first published, approximately fifty million men and women have quit smoking. Hip hip, hooray! And in some small way this little book has contributed to that life-saving progress.

# PREFACE

*Quit* was written for those millions of bright, intelligent people who have thought about kicking the cigarette habit, but needed a psychological "kick" to get them started. It is written especially for smokers who know they should quit smoking. Who know that cigarette smoking is harmful to their health, but reject as too painful any invitation to learn more about their awful addiction and take the steps that lead to quitting.

Smokers have the remarkable ability to "tune out" virtually all of the thousands of messages that suggest, many of them quite vividly, that cigarette smoking is dangerous to their health.

Day in and day out, smokers hear the message, but deny its relevance long enough for it to take root, to grow, to trigger a viable course of personal action. Many smokers, in fact, have unconsciously constructed an almost impenetrable wall that renders ineffective even the most purposeful efforts of friends and loved ones to convince them to break the smoking habit.

That's why this book was printed in this showy little package that looks just like a pack of cigarettes. I was hoping that someone you know, someone who's deeply concerned about your health, would give you this powerful short-course on quitting. And yet, the admonition would reach you in a package so cheery it would pierce the veil of hardened disinterest and actually produce positive action.

Well, this book is now in your hands, however it got there. And if you bought this volume for yourself, so much the better. It shows you love yourself enough to get serious about kicking the habit. But the big question is this: does it work? Can it help you quit smoking?

The answer: A definite "yes."

On the diminutive pages that follow, you'll find a powerful plan of such simplicity you can kick the cigarette habit in as little as one week! But, you've got to be willing to work at it and you've got to follow our simple, straightforward suggestions to the letter.

This book is designed to be carried with you and to take the place of your cigarettes. So carry it everywhere you go—in your purse, shirt pocket, suit coat, whatever! Soon, instead of reaching for a cigarette, you'll be reaching for helpful advice to delay smoking, and eventually avoid smoking, that next cigarette. Without self-torture. Without silly games.

And one more thing. Don't expect the slick verbiage that fattens some books. This book is blessedly short. You'll find no footnotes, appendices, glossaries, or bibliographies. What you'll find are just the facts—the plain unvarnished facts.

Likewise, I also have eliminated any instructions on how to read this book. The entire volume could be read in one sitting. For that reason, I won't ask you to read it at any prescribed rate: a chapter a day, twenty pages a week, etc. So read it any way you like. Just read it. And reread it. The first time right now.

The necessary steps are here. They have been proven time and time again, and by some of the leading health organizations, including the American Cancer Society, the American Lung Association, the American Heart Association, and others. The plan has worked for me and for millions of former smokers. And then, as now, it can work for you, too. Good luck.

# 1

## Quit: The System

One of the biggest obstacles to quitting smoking is that many plans involve lengthy and complicated formulas for accomplishing the task—including reading a book that is altogether too long. Some people lose interest halfway through the book. Others are tempted to smoke just because they're reading about smoking.

Yes, there are bigger books on the subject, but really, after all is said and done, the system is the thing. Boil it down to a few easy steps—bang, bang, bang—and nothing could be simpler.

Well, here are the easy steps—bang, bang, bang:

1. Determine why you want to quit smoking.
2. Rank your cigarettes for their importance to your lifestyle.
3. Gradually reduce your cigarette smoking.

4. Quit.
5. Guard yourself against a resumption of smoking.

These are the simple steps that this system requires. Naturally, you'll need detail to mold the steps of this program into a meaningful system for quitting, so let's get right to it.

## STEP ONE

***Determine why you want to quit smoking.*** We believe that your reasons for quitting could ultimately determine your quitting success.

# QUIT

If your reasons for quitting are flimsy, unconvincing, or contrived, they will never see you through what may be a difficult period ahead, regardless of what mettle of man or woman you think yourself to be.

We'll help you crystallize your thinking about non-smoking and your behavior around cigarettes. Perhaps you've never seriously thought about why you want to quit. But whether you have or not, we'll help you make some intelligent decisions toward living a fuller, healthier life.

## STEP TWO

***Rank your cigarettes.*** Each cigarette you smoke for several days will be rated on a scale of one to three for its importance to your lifestyle. Smoking is a very personal experience. And we continue this hazardous habit in the face of overwhelmingly damning evidence for a variety of reasons.

By rating your cigarettes, you will immediately determine what your smoking "bag" is, and how best to satisfy or reduce your obsession for cigarettes in other, less harmful ways.

## STEP THREE

***Reduce, steadily and gradually, your cigarette intake.*** Tapering your cigarette smoking is the real key to quitting for most people. Our bodies gradually got used to more and more cigarettes. And we can give them up the same gradual way that we learned how to smoke.

## STEP FOUR

***Call it Quits!*** Your Q-Day, the day you decide to call it quits, could be as near as a week from now (or from whenever you decide to start this program) or it may be much longer from now. It all depends on how much you smoke and how fast you want to quit. This is your program. Nobody can run it for you.

## STEP FIVE

*Quit for the long haul.* In this chapter, you'll learn about one of the most important steps in quitting smoking: Staying quit.

I'll acquaint you with some of the irrational thinking that has killed off many an attempt at continued nonsmoking.

As your Quit Day approaches, I

want to arm you with the important information you'll need to resist attacks of irrational thinking. I'll help you devise a plan of physical and mental exercises to help you guard against these deadly attacks.

On the brighter side, you'll find that in less than one week after you've stopped smoking completely, the tedium of cigarette preoccupation will begin to subside. You'll begin to lead the kind of healthful, zestful life that makes nonsmoking such a pleasure, so utterly worthwhile.

You will have a new sense of mastery over your life, a new feeling of freedom and control. And you'll be on your way to becoming free from cigarette slavery—hopefully forever.

And it's really as simple as that. There is no need to complicate or belabor these simple truths. So keep this little book in your breast pocket or purse and let's get on with it. Let's Quit!

# 2

# Why Quit?

One of the principal themes of this program is that it is easy to quit smoking, at least, temporarily. Alas, you may have done that several times already. And if not, certainly you have a number of friends and acquaintances who have been in and out of the smoking habit so often that they don't know whether they're coming or going.

While it is easy to quit, for several hours, a day, and even several weeks or months, it is more difficult to quit for any significant length of time—say two, five, or ten years.

And the imperceptible difference between those who succeed and those who do not often may be traceable not so much to the sincerity of their decision to quit or the validity of their reasons for quitting, but rather, to their strength and genuine acceptance of those reasons.

In the inevitable struggle between an intense cigarette craving and the long-range, but abstract benefit of a healthier life, the former always will endure when the commitment is shallow.

That subject will be pursued more fully in a later chapter. For now, it is important only to note that your reasons for quitting are unquestionably important. If you are to be successful at giving up cigarettes, your reasons for quitting must be forceful and compelling; your commitment must be deep and genuine.

So before discussing what goes wrong with our resolve, let's discuss some of your reasons for quitting smoking.

## Life or Death

There are any number of important reasons you may have for wanting to quit smoking cigarettes. In fact, the reason may stare you in the face every time you buy a pack of cigarettes and every time you "light up."

SURGEON GENERAL'S WARNING: Smoking causes lung cancer, heart disease, emphysema, and may complicate pregnancy.

The evidence that this is true is so overwhelming that it's almost unnecessary to document its credibility. Almost, but not quite.

There is no controversy about the facts. Thousands of studies have documented them. And all the major medical health agencies agree and even the major tobacco companies will now concede, cigarette smoking kills.

According to the U.S. Public Health Service Office on Smoking and Health, about 500,000 people die prematurely each year because of smoking. That's more than all the Americans killed in all of the wars the U.S. has ever fought. They die from lung cancer, heart disease, emphysema, and other illnesses.

Millions more, says the

American Lung Association, live on with crippled lungs and over-strained hearts.

## Lung Cancer

Cigarette smoking is the number one cause of lung cancer, according to the American Cancer Society. Each year, more than 100,000 smokers die in the U.S. from this disease. Smoking is responsible for almost ninety percent of lung cancers among men and more than seventy percent among women. Worse, when you get lung cancer, you're very likely to die from lung cancer.

It's ninety-two percent fatal among men; eighty-eight percent fatal among women.

The average cigarette smoker runs a risk of death from lung cancer ten times greater than the nonsmoker. If you started smoking as a teenager, the lung cancer rate zooms to nineteen times higher. And men who smoke more than a pack of cigarettes a day have about twenty times the lung cancer rate of nonsmokers.

The Cancer Society now says that lung cancer is also the number one cause of cancer deaths among women, for the first time in history, edging out breast cancer. Lung cancer among women has increased by 450 percent since 1950. At least 40,000 women will die from lung cancer this year.

Cigarette smokers also run a much higher risk of being struck by many other forms of cancer, including cancer of the mouth, larynx, and esophagus. Cigarette smoking is also associated with higher rates of cancer of the urinary bladder and kidney.

## Emphysema

Emphysema is one of several chronic obstructive pulmonary diseases that kills more than 80,000 men and women each year, and cigarette smoking causes eighty percent of those deaths. Emphysema, a disorder that both cripples and kills, is linked almost entirely with cigarette smoking, killing more than 30,000 persons each year.

Emphysema causes abnormal swelling and destruction of lung tissue. The physiological result is that smoking "thins" the air you breathe because your lungs can't do their job of extracting oxygen from the air and passing it on to the blood. It's like trying to breathe atop Mt. Everest.

Lungs maimed by emphysema eventually lose their elasticity. Breathing becomes a continuous, agonizing struggle. And there's little hope for significant recovery. Lung tissue destroyed by emphysema can never be replaced. Its slow, steady progression turns its victims into respiratory cripples, who spend agonizing years gasping for breath. Death, when it comes, is often the result of an overworked heart.

Cigarette smoking is also associated with higher rates of peptic ulcers, stomach disorders, and periodontal disease.

## Have A Heart

Smoking increases the death rate from heart attacks and strokes. At least 180,000 Americans die each year from cigarette-related cardio-vascular disease, the major cause of death among both males and females.

Middle-aged men who smoke heavily have a heart attack rate twice as high as that of nonsmokers. Women who smoke a pack a day are now five times more likely to suffer a heart attack.

Male smokers between forty-five and fifty-four years of age, have more than three times the death rates from heart attacks as nonsmokers. Between the ages of forty and fifty-nine, strokes kill nearly twice as many men who smoke as nonsmokers. Women smokers in the same age group have four times as many strokes as men.

Other studies show that death rates from heart attacks in men range from fifty to two hundred percent higher among cigarette smokers than nonsmokers, depending on age and the amount smoked.

Worse yet, smoking is another unnecessary risk for those people who are more susceptible to coronary artery disease, such as those with high blood pressure, high blood cholesterol, signs of hardening of the arteries, or a family history of heart attacks or strokes.

## Smoking and Pregnancy

Not only does your own health go up in smoke, but studies also show that smoking gravely affects the lives of the unborn.

Some fifteen million American adult women are of child-bearing age. Females who smoke during pregnancy have higher risks of miscarriages, stillbirths, placental abnormalities, and premature deliveries. Babies born to smokers are more likely to be underweight and suffer serious, sometimes fatal, respiratory illnesses. In fact, a former U.S. surgeon general reports that fetal and infant deaths increase by as much as twenty-eight to sixty percent in a small and selected sample of women who kept smoking during pregnancy.

## Death from Passive Smoke

You don't even have to be a cigarette smoker to die from smoking. The National Institutes of Health says smoke breathed by nonsmokers kills 5,000 people each year. Involuntary smoking also causes heart disease, aggravates asthmatic conditions, and impairs blood circulation.

Restaurant workers, for example, may be at least fifty percent more likely to get lung cancer due to second-hand smoke exposure. Closer to home, when a husband smokes, his nonsmoking wife doubles her chance of developing lung cancer. Nonsmoking wives of husbands who smoke have a thirty percent increased risk of lung cancer compared with women whose husbands don't smoke. Nonsmokers married to heavy smokers run two to three times the risk of lung cancer compared with those married to nonsmokers.

## Smoking Kills

The summary of all this, the bottom line if you please, is that "Cigarette smoking is dangerous to your health." And it says so on every pack of cigarettes you smoke. And the dangers increase the longer you smoke and the more you smoke. Study after study confirms what we know in our hearts to be true:

Cigarette smoking kills and cripples in more ways than most smokers readily admit.

## Begin Life Anew

By quitting smoking, you will immediately begin to look and feel better, healthier. In fact, in just twenty minutes after you quit, your blood pressure will drop and the temperature of your hands and feet will increase to normal.

In just twenty-four hours, your chance of heart attack decreases.

Three months after quitting, your circulation will improve and lung function can increase up to thirty percent.

In one year, your excess risk of coronary heart disease becomes half that of a smoker's.

After ten years as a nonsmoker, the lung cancer rate will approach about half that of a continuing smoker.

And after fifteen years of smoke-free living, your risk of coronary heart disease will be that of a nonsmoker.

Conversely, if you continue to smoke, you will increase your chances of contracting lung cancer, heart disease, emphysema, chronic bronchitis, and other cancerous and noncancerous diseases five, ten, and even twentyfold.

The medical reasons for quitting are many. The medical benefits of quitting are both immediate and long range. NOW is the time to quit.

## Give Yourself That Good Feeling

You may have many other health-related reasons for giving up smoking cigarettes. Food, for example, will probably taste remarkably better when you quit.

Your sense of smell will sharpen, improve. That hacking cough, that awful phlegm, those smoker's headaches, that foul breath, the telltale yellowing of the teeth and fingers—you can say good-bye to them all when you quit.

By giving up cigarettes, you will instantly invoke a program of being kind to your total body, including your heart, stomach, lungs, nose, and throat.

By comparison, most other reasons for giving up cigarettes become pale indeed. In fact, they may even become academic if you smoke long and hard enough. But

for now, they may be important to you so let's run through the list.

## Set A Good Example

You will no longer set a bad example for your children, your spouse, friends, and associates and befoul their air with the stench of your cigarette smoke. And don't underestimate the effect of your smoking presence. Studies show that if one parent smokes, their children are twice as likely to smoke. And if both parents smoke, their children are three times more likely to smoke.

## Newfound Wealth

New wealth will jingle in your jeans because you won't be spending the vast sums on this empty habit. Multiply for yourself what you're sending up in smoke each year. I know you'll be surprised. Many former smokers find that giving up cigarettes is just like giving themselves a raise of $100–$150 a month, and maybe more.

Certain insurance companies offer reduced auto and life insurance rates for the nonsmoker. The same is true for health insurance companies that may actually decline to underwrite insurance on chronic smokers. Perhaps this too is an extra reason for you to kick the smoking habit.

Still, having extra money compares little with having extra life. At least I hope so. But I'm not about to disparage anyone's reason or reasons for quitting smoking. If it gets you to quit smoking, it's a good reason.

## Freedom at Last

Your reasons for quitting may be none of these, but rather, a deep-seated need to rid yourself of an addictive habit.

Many people feel this way. They tire of having to continually "stock up" on their chemical dependence—cigarettes—every day, every night, every weekend, year in, year out.

They want that feeling of freedom that comes from forever forgetting about matches, lighters, ashtrays, cigarettes, and all that mess. They want to move about in this world unmindful of smoking rules, regulations, and punishing prohibitions that today are everywhere.

The nonsmoking public is coming down hard on smokers. The decision by the Government Service Administration to prohibit smoking in most federal buildings is just the tip of the iceberg. That ruling left hundreds of thousands of workers in thousands of government buildings looking for a place to light up. Without a doubt, smokers are becoming segregated from society.

When you quit smoking, you can forget about these kinds of considerations forever, except of course, when you pause to remember how bad it used to be.

Do you remember when you trudged ten blocks to the corner drugstore in subzero weather to get your smokes—only to find the store shuttered and dark? And you returned home empty-handed to scrounge the ashtrays for smoke-able butts but your spouse had already dumped them into the garbage. And now, here you are, digging through the garbage to satisfy your habit. And the coffee grounds made them too soggy to smoke. Do you remember?

Well, many of us remember situations in which we became desperate for a smoke and broke laws and good sense to satisfy our addiction. And many of us rank slavery to the cigarette habit as one of the chief reasons for quitting.

But again, perhaps the health

and welfare reasons are unimportant to you. That's fair enough. And while it's terribly difficult to argue about the reliability or validity of the wealth of research studies that prove cigarette smoking causes death and disease, I am not asking you to accept these findings as your reasons for quitting.

## List Your Reasons

But what are your reasons? To find out, I want you to make your own personal list of reasons why you would like to join the more than fifty million former cigarette smokers in this country.

Right now, turn to the pages at the back of this book and start listing your reasons for quitting. Take as complete an inventory as possible and list all your reasons, regardless of how trivial some may seem.

When you have listed at least ten, rank them in order for their importance. Perhaps the health consideration is most important. Maybe you're more concerned about setting a better example for your children.

When you have your reasons prioritized, take the three most

important ones and put them on a card or slip of paper that's small enough to fit behind the cellophane of your pack of cigarettes. On the reverse side, list the remainder of your reasons. Keep them there. They now will serve important and useful purposes.

This list is your permanent reference card. Every time you reach for a smoke, read this list. I want you to memorize the list. I want you to roll these reasons around in your mind again and again.

It may be helpful for you to phrase your reasons for quitting in language less abstract than statistical comparisons or deathly prose. One former smoker I know, for example, merely stated his health-related reason for quitting by noting he want to live long enough to spend another summer enjoying his favorite pastime, boating. Another jotted down that he wanted "freedom from slavery."

You can do the same. Write down why you want to live a longer, healthier life.

Here are some examples:

- *I want to set a good example for my children*

# WHY QUIT?

- *I want to be around to enjoy my retirement*

- *I want to save $1000 a year to buy some new clothes*

- *I don't want to be a slave any longer*

- *I don't want cigarette-cough anymore*

- *I love my life too much to smoke*

- *Cigarette smoking is offensive*

- *I want to be free*

- *I don't want to die any earlier than I have to*

Whatever reason for quitting appeals to you—really appeals to you—write it down and read both sides of your list, the Top Three and your secondary reasons, often.

Think about putting some of your reasons on heavy cards and placing them in various spots in your home or office where you're most likely to see and read them. Perhaps you could place one next to your office telephone, or near the place where you most frequently smoke when you're at home. You'd be surprised at how deeply an impact these little reminders have on your cigarette intake.

Remember that in the crush of daily events, our minds often get swept away with the tedium, the routine, of just *living*. The mundane crowds out thoughts of our goals and aspirations.

Don't let that happen to you.

The important thing to remember here is that, when you quit smoking, be fully aware of your reasons for quitting as much as you can. I want your reasons to be crystal clear and on your mind at all times, and certainly every time you have a cigarette. It's your first step in joining the growing majority of Americans who have made their decision to kick the cigarette habit.

# 3

## What's Your Bag?

Many smokers think they know all of the answers about their habit and continue to smoke, believing it's too tough, maybe even impossible, to give up cigarettes forever.

But smokers who sit down and examine the relationship they have developed with cigarettes discover they already possess the power, in the form of knowledge, to give up the smoking habit.

Most smokers, for example, are surprised to learn that much of their smoking can be described as an "unconscious" act that can easily, almost effortlessly, be given up at any time—completely and forever.

In fact, the cigarettes you smoke that really "turn you on" are very few in number and can be given up more easily if you know why they turn you on. And that's what this chapter is all about.

Starting tomorrow, or today if you like, I want you to "keep score" of the cigarettes you smoke. I want you to determine for yourself what kind of smoker you are, what kind of cigarettes turn you on, or turn you off, slow you down, speed you up, satisfy your urges, or occupy your more creative or organizational moments.

To effectively quit smoking, it is helpful to know what sort of social, or non-social, situations enhance or even help create your smoking pleasure.

When you know this, you can start breaking your smoking habit down into understandable components and eliminating them one by one.

For the most part, I have found that it is unimportant to know why we first started smoking. But it is important to know something about the payoffs that keep us smoking.

## Why You Smoke

Smokers "light up" for a variety of reasons—not just one—and in answer to many different situations. The American Cancer Society, for example, suggests that there are at least a half-dozen definable reasons why we smoke.

### *The Need*

Certainly, one of the most compelling reasons we smoke is the actual craving, the addiction to the nicotine. Long denied by tobacco company executives, smoking is now regarded by virtually all authorities as an *addictive* habit. The smoker who begins craving a cigarette soon after he or she puts one out is controlled by a deep-seated psychological and physiological habit.

This kind of smoker will feel uncomfortable, sometimes even panicky, without a cigarette. And she or he will go to almost any length to get a cigarette—walking a mile or sifting the garbage included.

The pleasure one gets from smoking these cigarettes is very fleeting. Like an alcoholic or drug-dependent person, this smoker must constantly feed his habit.

What's important about these cigarettes is that they satisfy a very real need. Therefore, they will be much more difficult to give up than other cigarettes that do not satisfy an addictive need.

That's why most smokers experience *withdrawal* when they quit smoking. This discomfort is not unlike the withdrawal that accompanies the removal of other drugs, although not usually as severe.

We've all heard stories from former smokers about the withdrawal symptoms they encountered; their bouts with grouchiness, short tempers, nervousness, and the like. These all are symptoms of nicotine withdrawal, a circumstance that, in itself, is a symptom of the addiction.

A number of smokers that I know have endured these cravings and the associated withdrawal symptoms. After an agonizing but successful effort at quitting, most vowed never again to smoke, chiefly because they didn't want to endure the same discomfort and ordeal again.

## *Mindless Habit*

The second kind of cigarettes we smoke are those we light up in mindless habit—and I do mean mindless. Often, we light up so automatically we are stunned to discover a cigarette already burning. Sometimes we are even embarrassed to find not one, but two cigarettes burning in different parts of the house.

These "habit" cigarettes are relatively easy to give up immediately, once we become aware of the habit pattern. They are easy to give up because they usually produce so little satisfaction.

This brings us back to our plan of listing—and then reading—our reasons for quitting *every time* we reach for a cigarette. Often, just *reading* our list of reasons is enough to forego smoking; just this once. When we become aware of just how many of these unconscious little cigarettes go up in smoke, oftentimes "unsmoked," it's easy to give them up. Just being aware of the habit is enough to kick the habit.

### *Where There's Stress There's Smoke*

Other smokers say they puff when they are under stress or pressure. This smoker seeks to reduce or eliminate certain feelings of stress, fear, distress, guilt, or discomfort by lighting up. This smoker can easily quit—until the pressure and the tension mount. When that happens, they find themselves inventing excuses to start smoking again...at least until the pressure subsides. When things are going poorly, this smoker will find it difficult to resist—and easy to rationalize it—just this once.

### *Double Your Pleasure*

Conversely, some smokers are into the nicotine habit because it really turns them on—particularly in conjunction with some other event that makes them feel good. Many smokers are pretty keen about this aspect of their smoking habit and many of their life's events are associated with smoking. Sex and a smoke. Dinner and a smoke.

Coffee and a smoke. Booze and a smoke, and so on.

The fact is that most smokers honestly do, at times, feel good when they smoke. And those who feel this way are likely to quit smoking only when they honestly believe that the pleasure might be overshadowed, at some point in their lives, by the pain from smoking transgressions of the past.

Unfortunately for the most of us, that pain and suffering from the diseases and ailments associated with cigarette smoking are as abstract as they are presently removed. And for many smokers, giving up that pleasure for the abstract benefits of *not* smoking will probably be difficult.

### *The Sensual Smoker*

Of all the reasons for continuing to smoke, one of the weakest is the kick some smokers get out of just "handling" their cigarettes. For some, the touching, feeling, fondling, lighting up, and touch to the lips is half the thrill of inhaling the smoke.

I suspect this "benefit" has, more or less, grown up with the habit. And if you're one of those who admittedly likes to toy with cigarettes, you'll be greatly relieved on your Quit Day to find some other substitute, a pencil or whatever, to fidget with.

## *We Are All Different*

Actually, there is a bit of each of these smokers in all of us and in varying degrees. The problem is to find out what kind of smoker you are and put that information to good use when it's your time to quit.

So starting right now, I want you to become aware of your smoking habit. On the pages at the end of this book, start making notes of (1) the time of day when you smoke each cigarette; and (2) what role this cigarette plays in your smoking life. That is, determine for yourself just what kind of need it satisfies for you.

Was it a cigarette smoked under tension? Was it a "relaxing" cigarette like those smoked after a morning cup of coffee? Was it just one of the cigarettes you smoked out of sheer habit and could easily have done without? Did the smoke serve some other purpose?

Not only do I want you to determine for yourself exactly what sort of cigarette satisfaction you get from smoking, I also want you to determine the importance of each cigarette you smoke to your lifestyle.

For simplicity sake, I want you to rate each smoke on a scale of one to three; one being the *least* important, and three the *most* important.

Chances are, regardless of the number of cigarettes you smoke each day, you'll have many more "ones" than you thought possible. In other words, you can easily cut down your smoking intake (something I'll be asking you to do in the next step) just by eliminating those cigarettes that mean little to your hard-core reasons for smoking. Again, you'll be surprised at how many cigarettes this can be.

But the cigarettes I'm most concerned about are those "threes." Not only are these cigarettes more difficult to eliminate, they'll also give you the most trouble when you begin to give up smoking.

These are the cigarettes that may start that negative thinking that produces mental sentences like these: "Is this really worth it?" Or, "I've just *got* to have a cigarette right now. I can always continue my program *after* this smoke. One little cigarette won't hurt, right?"

For now, though, all I want you to do is keep close track of what goes on in your head each time you light up. What sort of a need does each cigarette satisfy, when do you smoke it, and how important is it to your smoking lifestyle?

## *Your One-Week Test Drive*

You'll want to keep these records for at least a week. By the end of seven days, you'll likely have engaged in most of the routine situations of your smoking life. Certainly you'll have a pretty good handle on what sort of smok-

er you are and how best to start
cutting down.

And one more thing. Starting
today, I want you to **stop carrying
cigarettes with you.** Instead, carry
this book. I know that if you really
want a cigarette, you can always find
one. But in the meantime, carry this
book where you normally carried
your cigarettes. It's a great substitute.

# 4

## Countdown

Now that you know more about your smoking behavior and the type of "situation cigarettes" that are important to your smoking lifestyle, you can begin the process of gradually cutting down, of quitting smoking.

Notice that I said gradually.

While a few smokers might benefit from going "cold turkey," the vast majority of smokers will be more successful in their efforts if they eliminate their dependence on cigarettes gradually.

It's not my idea of a "method" to send the world crashing down on the smoker some dark, gloomy day. That's not the way to give up a habit that's taken you years to develop.

Instead, I've fashioned a method that lets you quit smoking one cigarette at a time, quickly, easily, and painlessly.

Our bodies, after all, have gradually become accustomed to the increasingly greater insult of cigarette smoke and tar as our cigarette habit has become more deeply ingrained. As our level of cigarette tolerance grows, so does our level of addictive cigarette intake.

Most smokers began with just a cigarette or two a day and gradually worked their way up to a pack of cigarettes or more each day. Now that you are at a pack-a-day or better level, it makes much more sense to back down from the habit the same way you got there, a cigarette at a time.

And that's just what I am now asking you to do.

## The Countdown

Starting today, and for as long as it takes, you are going to quit smoking one cigarette at a time. It makes little difference how many cigarettes you now smoke. You may be smoking a half-a-pack a week or a carton a day. But you are going to get rid of them, one by one, or faster. You can choose the cigarettes you wish to eliminate and you can choose the order in which you want to get rid of them.

Your goal in this step is to eliminate at least one cigarette each day until you have reduced your smoking to three or fewer cigarettes each day. At that point, it's time to quit altogether. And by then, your body and your mind are ready for this important step.

I don't care if the cigarette you quit each day has been ranked as a three or a one, just so you cut out one each day, *every day*.

I don't care if you eliminate all of your morning cigarettes, all of your evening cigarettes, every other cigarette, every third or fourth cigarette, just so you eliminate one cigarette each day.

I don't care if you get up later each day or go to bed earlier each day, just so you reach the goal: one day, one less cigarette.

Chances are, the first few days will see you eliminate more than just one a day. Some smokers can cut out all of their "unconscious," habit cigarettes in just a few days.

As a matter of fact, many smokers make rather dramatic reductions in their cigarette intake the first few days. But a word of caution here: huge reductions are neither necessary nor are they necessarily desirable. All I ask is one cigarette less each day.

Some former smokers I know were extremely successful in alternating between giving up a difficult cigarette and an easy one—a three and a one. Others had good luck starting to smoke a bit later each day.

But you be the judge. This is your program. Cut out the ones you want to, the ones you feel comfortable going without. It's the goal that's important, not how you get there. So make it easy on yourself if you like. Just make sure you make it to the finish line.

There are a lot of little ways you can make it easy on yourself, too.

Right now, turn to your ranking pages and reread your results. Look for *trends* in your smoking habit. Select those situations and periods of the day when you do most of your smoking.

Then, start a plan in your mind as to which of those cigarette situations you'd like to go after and eliminate. Like a military operation or thoughtful business plan, you can plot strategy on how to win the smoking war, one cigarette battle at a time.

Most smokers I know, for example, smoke a cigarette after every meal. That might be three definable smoking situations for possible elimination.

How about your coffee break? That's two or three more smoking situations you can consider eliminating.

You probably had a couple of smokes before breakfast. How about getting rid of one of them?

Study your ranking pages. Define the situations you wish to work on and then dig in. Again, it doesn't matter which cigarette you eliminate today . . . just so you eliminate at least one.

To help you carry out your attack, I've listed some situations, some self-helps to get the ball rolling. These ideas have worked for many former smokers and they can work for you.

## Tips To Taper

1. Don't carry cigarettes with you. Carry only this book. And read it when the urge to smoke strikes.

2. Put your cigarettes in out-of-the-way places . . . in the basement, the attic, in someone else's desk, in your file cabinet, in the medicine cabinet. Put them anywhere so they are out of sight, and hopefully, out of mind.

3. Change brands. If you smoke a filter, change to a non-filter. If you smoke a menthol, switch to a regular.

4. If smoking while drinking coffee or other beverage fits your smoking lifestyle, try cutting back on these drinks—just for now. Eliminating your lunch-time coffee, for example, could be the elimination of today's cigarette (and besides, you could do without the caffeine).

5. Begin smoking a little later each day. For example, delay that first cigarette until after you shower. Then after you get dressed. Then

after breakfast. Then after you get to work. And so on.

6. Quit smoking a little earlier each day. First after your evening snack. Then after your late news. Then after dinner, and so on.

7. Take long walks immediately after your meals—purposefully leaving your cigarettes behind. You can't smoke what you don't have. And the exercise is a great way to reduce the tension and stress associated with quitting smoking.

8. Alternate between giving up a morning, an afternoon, and an evening cigarette.

9. Give up smoking in certain places. For instance, never smoke while watching television news. Or, never light up while you're on the telephone.

10. Stock up on cigarette substitutes: mints, candies, and the like. Then look for cigarette situations in which you can pop a mint into your mouth instead of a cigarette.

11. Every time you reach for a cigarette, read your list of reasons for quitting. This step alone can often delay, and then eliminate, your cigarette for that day.

12. Put away your ashtrays, lighter, and matches, so you'll have to hunt them up every time you smoke. Sometimes it won't be worth the hassle and you'll have eliminated another cigarette.

13. Try to put yourself into "No Smoking" situations and places—no smoking sections in restaurants, and other public places, in libraries, bathtubs, courtrooms, churches, synagogues, airplanes, etc.

14. While you're at it, try out new situations, new places to eat, shop, etc. Newness gets you out of the rut of things, and it's a

chance to build new, clean habits.

15. Delay, just for now, smoking that next cigarette.
16. Give up smoking on your way to work.
17. Give up smoking on your way home from work.
18. Give up smoking in your car.
19. Give up your morning coffee break.
20. "Accidentally" leave your cigarettes at home when you leave for work each day.
21. Take a bus to work instead of a car.
22. Instead of having a cigarette following dinner, go brush your teeth.

23. Try to smoke no more than one cigarette each hour, for this hour only.
24. Give up coffee for lunch, and the cigarette you normally smoke with it.
25. Give up smoking while using the telephone.
26. Give up smoking while you are reading the newspapers.
27. Take few and smaller drags from each cigarette you smoke.

These are just a few of the ways in which you can gradually cut down your smoking intake. You can use as many as you wish. And you are free to develop ideas of your own to help you cut down on cigarettes.

## There's No Turning Back

There is another crucial part of this step. Once you eliminate a cigarette, you can't go back to it. That's right. It's over and out. You can't return. So, if you give up the cigarette you always had with your morning coffee break, I want you to forever stop smoking that cigarette. If you decide to begin smoking at a later and later time each day, *do not* revert back to an earlier time of smoking.

The Quit Plan seeks to develop periods during your day when your body is free from cigarette smoke, free from addictive nicotine. As these periods get longer and longer, several good things happen.

First of all, by quitting cigarettes one at a time, you'll learn important, new information about your smoking habits and how to eliminate them.

Secondly, you'll develop a whole new repertoire of skills to cope with the problems associated with certain aspects of your smoking addiction.

Thirdly, you'll earn a growing

sense of pride and increased self-esteem. It's a great feeling, a terrific sense of power, to realize that you no longer need to search out a smoking section in a restaurant to carry on your habit. Now you can sit anywhere you please because you have become master of that part of your smoking habit.

It's a nice feeling to know that you don't *have* to light up when you finish a meal or enjoy a second cup of coffee—you have the power to say NO! I think you'll be surprised at how quickly you can form new, nonsmoking habits after just a few days of "doing without."

And what's more important, each component cigarette that you eliminate from your smoking habit will inspire a sense of renewed self-confidence over this habit.

Lastly, and perhaps most important, giving up cigarette after cigarette gradually reduces your addictive *dependence* on cigarettes.

Most smokers, for example, are very pleasantly surprised to learn that their smoking habit is largely defined by a few, "I've-got-to-have-it" smokes interspersed by a much larger number of cigarettes that offer no real felt satisfaction. Most would have believed it was impossible to eliminate the vast majority of cigarettes they smoke without noticeable disruption to their lives. What's more, kicking each individual component of your habit creates fresh assurance that additional, even more difficult cigarettes can be given up tomorrow and the next day.

## Your Progress

As the days slip by and the number of cigarettes you smoke dwindles, you'll develop a new sense of pride in your accomplishment.

The withdrawal symptoms such as dizziness, increased irritability, etc., have been significantly reduced, if they were ever a problem at all.

You're now in better shape to deal with new, nonsmoking situations because you have already confronted, and successfully controlled, a portion of your cigarette habit at various times throughout the day.

If you have not made steady progress in cutting down your smoking intake, you should read Chapter 2 again and determine if now is the right time for you to quit. If you're not one hundred percent in the program, it's doubtful you will succeed.

# QUIT

And at this point in your program, some sharp decisions have to be made. It's now time to take a stand for Quitting Success.

# 5

# The Enemy Within

In an earlier chapter, I acknowledged that many people have tried to quit smoking and have not succeeded. In fact, most people have tried to quit *several* times without succeeding. Sure, they quit for a few days or weeks, only to take up smoking again.

What happened? How did these people, whose resolves in the beginning seemed so firm, so virtuous, so steadfast, crumble under the weight of becoming "masters of their fate and slaves to none?"

How did they begin anew to increase their chances for an earlier grave as surely as taking a daily dose of poison—which is exactly what cigarette smoking is. How is it that, without benefit or excuse of childhood innocence, did they, with all their maturity and intelligence, start smoking again?

Perhaps we can find the answer by looking at what happens, both in

the beginning and even in later
months and years, to those who try
to give up smoking cigarettes.

## When You Quit

The first thing you'll notice when
you quit smoking is a sudden and
all-encompassing preoccupation with
cigarettes and smoking.

In previous months and years,
you gave the habit virtually no
thought at all. In the past few days
or weeks, smoking has carved out a
larger portion of your thinking day.
But when you quit, almost *all* of
your thoughts will be on smoking.

The first day, it will seem as if hardly a minute goes by when you are not thinking about or perhaps wishing you could smoke a cigarette. And sometimes, hardly a minute *will* pass when you're not absorbed with thoughts of smoking.

Virtually everyone who quits smoking experiences this obsession. Some for just a few days. Others for weeks, even months.

Cigarette smoking preoccupation is one of the reasons why a number of excellent self-help groups have sprung up around the country. They provide the newly-reformed nonsmoker with someone to talk him over the early rough spots, to take his mind off smoking, and to offer camaraderie and shared experiences during these troublesome episodes.

Again, I recommend that if you have trouble with this problem and it threatens your success, then by all means, join a self-help group.

Perhaps even a nonsmoking or former smoking friend can help and may well be your salvation. Give it some serious consideration.

The preoccupation is bad enough. But with it, many nonsmoking tenderfoots experience waves of irrationality that can distort, dismember, and then dissolve their willpower. Worse yet, the irrationality of such thoughts often goes undetected and this thinking comes down to us as perfectly cogent and acceptable.

For example, if your original reason for quitting smoking was that you believed it was harmful to your health, you may come to rationalize, as the cigarette urge strikes you particularly hard, that smoking isn't all *that* harmful. Such a subtle shift in emphasis and you have an entirely new premise to continue your dirty old ways.

If you formerly believed that

you might someday die of a need-less, cigarette-induced lung cancer, you might remind yourself, during a bout with cigarette craving, that there are millions of people who smoked and lived to ripe old ages without ever so much as a hint of cigarette-caused illness.

If you resolved that your *heavy* smoking was harmful to your health, you may then come to believe, when under attack of nico-tine desire, that you're not smoking nearly so much anymore, that a few cigarettes a day never hurt anyone.

And the rationalizations go on and on, bridled only by your imagi-

nation to create perfectly credible
"reasons" to continue behavior that
you previously had come to believe
was perfectly unacceptable.

Just give a listen and see if you
hear yourself saying:

*Cigarettes expensive? It's only
money.*

*I quit this time. I can always do
it again.*

*The tension is unbearable.*

*It isn't worth the hassle.*

*I can always do it later.*

*Just this one time.*

*I'm just too weak.*

*I can't.*

Does all of this sound familiar?

It's as if there were really two of us, warring within. One side does the rationalizing. The other half still believes, although ever more faintly, that this is the time to quit and for the most compelling reason: To Live.

Who wins?

You, the nonsmoker does, if you are prepared, committed, and honest.

## Your Commitment

Much of the mental gymnastics that occur when we attempt to give up cigarettes happens on the uncon-

111

scious level and is inappropriate for discussion here.

I don't pretend to be a psychiatrist or a psychologist. But I am firmly convinced of this solid fact: when you are *aware* of the games the mind can play when the body is faced with a cigarette craving, you are much better able to defend yourself in the skirmishes that can, and undoubtedly will, occur.

That's why it's a useful exercise to rehearse some of these mental games beforehand and think about some of the irrationalities that could ultimately weaken your resolve.

For example, let's assume for the moment that you are giving up cigarettes because you firmly believe them to be detrimental to your health and that you may someday die an early death if you don't give them up right now. You also know, of course, that this fact continues to be true, despite any wavering of belief or commitment on your part.

But when the craving for a cigarette strikes you so badly that your hair hurts, don't be surprised to hear those rationalizations popping into your head almost as freely and uncontrollably as hallucinogenic

113

thoughts. From nowhere come these irrationalities. Almost without notice you could hear yourself starting to say, "This just isn't worth the hassle."

At that moment, you had better shout right back to yourself, "You damn well better believe it's worth the hassle because I know very well that thousands of people die unnecessarily each year from cigarette smoking and I know full well that I, just as easily as my smoking neighbor, may be next in line for the mortician's table. Quitting is hard. Dying is harder."

What's more, you can add, this

*has* to be a habit worth quitting if only because any habit that distorts and controls my thinking as this one does *must* be a habit well worth kicking.

And when you hear one part of your mind saying to another, "I can always quit later," you had better haul yourself up short by contradicting, "This habit is so deadly that my later might well be more painful than anything I'm experiencing right now."

And when you hear yourself talking about too much tension to bear, remind yourself that a little tension is nothing compared to a *great* deal of needless suffering, that you can probably endure almost any tension for a little while without a cigarette.

Or if one of your reasons for quitting was because you wanted to stop being a slave to a habit and now you suddenly find yourself debating that premise, remember: there is very little freedom in smoking yourself to death.

The proposition of giving up smoking is as serious as that. And it is just as deadly an issue today as it will be for years to come.

Even years from now, when you say to yourself that "a cigarette or two won't hurt just this once," a little bell ought to start ringing in your head. Right then and there, you should start reminding yourself of a quit-smoking program you read a long time ago that warned you of times like these, occasions when you seriously entertained the notion of starting to smoke again.

I hope that bell will be loud enough to remind you of your original reasons for quitting, whatever they were. And remember, if they were good enough for you then, they're certainly good enough for you now.

So remember, it is important for

you to be prepared with the knowledge that: (1) at times, perhaps at many times, you will feel the urge to smoke; (2) certain irrational thinking such as that I have discussed will often accompany that craving; (3) by being *aware* of what's going on, a little bell will go off in your head; and (4) you will be able to "see through" the temporary superficiality of your thinking and maintain your nonsmoking headway, regardless of how short, or how long, your period of freedom from cigarettes may be.

So right now, give your reasons for quitting a really good going over. Think *now* of the ways in which you might later be trying to talk yourself out of your good resolves...and into an earlier grave.

Memorize the replies that you will be making to yourself if this stinking kind of thinking should begin.

## What Quitting Is All About

Here's something else I want you to think about. After years of observing, teaching, and writing about behavior change, I am convinced that most quitters have the mistaken idea about what "quitting" is all about.

You've no doubt witnessed that quitting smoking is—most of the time—rather easy. Quitting is, in reality, long periods of effortless non-smoking interspersed by a few cravings that are so powerful they create tremendous inner disruptions.

When all is said and done, "quitting smoking" is about what you do and what actions you take (or fail to take) when these urges spring upon you. And the actions you take are in turn directly the result of your commitment to the nonsmoking lifestyle. In other words, when the urge to smoke strikes, you can't sit there like a bump on a log, you have to *do* something. If you sit back and allow the craving to consume you, without doing anything, your quitting smoking program is doomed.

## Your Commitment

If your commitment to giving up cigarettes is sufficiently genuine, you will do whatever is necessary, however troublesome, to protect your nonsmoking freedom.

Maybe you will have to seek help at times, a friend, a nonsmoking neighbor, a self-help group, an anonymous internet chat-room acquaintance. Maybe you'll read these chapters again, and again, and again. Maybe you'll have to read other quit smoking books to help you succeed.

Think and plan *now* of what you're going to do when the craving hits, as it most assuredly will. Are you going to take a walk? Call a friend? Soak in a bathtub? If you wait until the urge to smoke strikes, it may well be too late.

Again, if your *commitment* is there, you'll do whatever is necessary to quit smoking. If your commitment isn't there, then perhaps you'll find completing even the first step of this program too much of a challenge.

So start rehearsing right now. Really. Think of all the sentences, all the stinking thinking, that may be racing through your mind when the going gets rough. Learn them by heart. And when the urge strikes, you'll be successfully prepared.

# 6

## Setting Your Quit Day

It is now the moment of truth—that point at which the "quitters" will be galloping off toward a new healthier, freer life, while the nonquitters will inexorably slide backward in their losing race with smoking's deadly statistics.

Does that sound a little heavy? Perhaps. But I know full well—and so do you—that giving up cigarettes is as important as life and death.

Because of the gravity of the decision, a few important points are now in order.

## A Day At A Time

The most important point you can remember in your efforts to quit smoking is this:

*You can only quit for*
*ONE DAY at a time.*

Let me repeat that. You can only quit smoking for one day at a time.

And worrying about whether you'll make it through tomorrow or next week or the rest of your life is a fruitless, damaging exercise.

You can quit only for this moment. So let the rest of the moments of what will become the rest of your life worry about themselves.

Many quitters, in fact, concern themselves not with a *day* at a time, but rather, an hour at a time, or even a minute at a time.

And if that sounds foolish, just remember that we receive our lives only a moment at a time so it is impossible to live in the future. So let's not worry about it.

Take it as it comes. Worry only about what's here and now.

## This Is Your Plan

Another point to remember is that not everyone gives up smoking the first time around. Many former smokers tried to quit several times, and did not, before finally garnering the experience, strength, and commitment to give up this habit for good.

On the other hand, this is no time for a cop-out, for a half-hearted attempt designed only to make yourself feel good, or reduce the heat from a nagging spouse, or soothe a bad case of the screaming guilties.

Sure, you can decide that perhaps you'd rather wait a while before really calling it quits. And that's okay with me. It's your heart. It's your lungs. It's your life. You can do whatever you want with them.

But let's be sensible. Really sensible. It could be now or never. So choose wisely.

## You Are Ready

I have now given you the ammunition you'll need to successfully

129

wage war on your Quit Day, whenever you choose it to be. I have helped you determine, first of all, why you want to quit smoking.

There were scores of important reasons you could have chosen from, but if you are like most, you decided to start giving your body every possible chance to reach a healthy old age.

God knows there are too many ways to meet an early death without purposely adding a few more.

I have tried to impress upon you the importance of carefully selecting and memorizing your reasons for giving up cigarettes so that you are ready to counter some of the wayward thoughts that will flit through your mind in the weeks and months ahead.

I know that these reasons may well undergo considerable emotional scrutiny, sometimes with a mind-set more predisposed to acquiescing to, rather than fighting off, a powerful cigarette craving.

For that reason, I set aside a chapter to help you prepare for what could be a critical onslaught of stinking thinking that could kill your efforts to live a longer life.

I have also watched as your cigarette intake has dwindled from double-digits to as few as two or three. And now that you can count them on one hand, it's time to count them out altogether.

You have determined for yourself what kind of cigarette smoker you are, and what kind of situations trigger smoking, the kind of situations you'll want to avoid when your Quit Day arrives.

The score cards you have been keeping will give you invaluable insight into which days are better, which are worse, for your debut into the nonsmoking world. Not only that, they will indicate what times of the day you'll need to be extra careful, when to slow down, and when to relax.

Turn again to those scorecard pages and take another inventory. Perhaps you'll find that the tension is just a bit too much to deal with during the working week and you might be better served starting your program to quit on a weekend.

Or, the opposite might be true. Some smokers have found that weekend activities and the drinking of alcoholic beverages might tip the scale in consideration of a weekday start.

Some find it is easier to quit during a vacation when they can pack

133

themselves away in some remote spot—away from cigarettes altogether. Naturally, if this is November and your vacation is not until July, better think again.

Still others seem to face no barriers whatsoever. They sail through the quitting experience with little or no trouble at all—even without altering their lifestyle. They plunge headlong into this new experience. They want to be exposed to the kind of temptation they will have to face on a regular, nonsmoking basis.

Naturally, all smokers who quit will eventually have to get into their regular scheme of things. So, this may not be a bad way to go.

But you be the judge. This is your program, to the very end.

And the end is near. You now have cut your cigarette habit down to a precious few per day. You already have gone through much, if not most, of the withdrawal associated with slimming down your cigarette habit.

At this point, you may wish to continue your gradual cigarette reduction 3-2-1, or you may elect to call it quits right now.

Many former smokers thought the remainder of the one-a-day

reduction much more trouble than it was worth. They were ready to quit and they knew it. They decided enough is enough. Let's call it quits right now.

You may also strongly consider the possibility of joining a quit smoking clinic of some kind. Right now is a good time to join. Just like many other self-help groups, sharing your quitting experiences could be just the therapy you need to make your efforts at quitting painlessly successful. There is something about sharing your problems that makes the problem itself easier to solve. And this is just as true for overeating and drinking as it is for smoking.

Whatever you think will work for you is okay. Just pick a day and a date to suit your pleasure. But pick the date *today*.

And remember, when you set your Quit Day, it's not the last cigarette you will ever smoke. It's just for *today* that you have to quit smoking, just one day at a time. And that's an option—a commitment—you can renew one day at a time, for the rest of your life.

# 7

## Your Quit Day

This is it. This is the day when you call it quits to smoking and begin to live a new, healthier life. You may want to make a big deal out of your Quit Day. You may want to do just the opposite, as if Quit Day were just another ordinary day. It's a personal decision. Do what's best for you.

You may feel that telling your family, friends, and associates will enhance your chances for success because you've made a commitment to others—people you don't want to let down.

This may be particularly true if your family and friends are supportive of your attempt and likely to be understanding, or at least *tolerant* of your first-day jitters or irritability. Maybe they, too, are former smokers who can offer you valuable help and assistance in your quest to "take charge."

Other nonsmoking wannabes, however, are troubled by a needless "fear of failure" that they believe can be reduced by keeping their plans a secret. They think it's easier to quit if no one knows about their attempt—or any failure that could follow.

## You're A Winner

A few words are in order at this point about the success or failure of your effort at giving up smoking. Many smokers feel that when they quit smoking, they are exercising "willpower" and that, if they fail to give up smoking, they become failures.

*Au contraire.* I indicated elsewhere in this book that it is not "willpower" that spells the difference in quitting cigarettes. Rather, it is our *commitment* to learn new behavior to replace old.

To put it another way, "willpower" is what gets you to try giving up cigarettes. It is "commitment" that gives you the complete follow-through to see your act to a successful conclusion.

Maybe this is one of the problems of those who try to quit smoking. From their vantage points, they cannot "see" the entire scenario of their attempt, or attempts, at quitting smoking, and therefore cannot see that at a later date, they actually did quit smoking.

As usual, hindsight is 20/20. And life would be a great deal more orderly if we knew, in advance, how everything was going to turn out.

More than one smoker I know has wished he could have peered into his crystal ball to see if he really made it.

## Your First Day

When you wake up on Quit Day, you may be overcome with a fear that "I can never have another cigarette again."

Put that thought out of your mind at once! Replace it with this one: "I will, just for today, or just for this minute of my life, give up smoking."

Remember that you only receive your life one day at a time. And it's a far easier thing to give up smoking for just one day, than it is for the rest of your life.

And I have some additional thoughts and ideas for your first few days, some of which you may have heard before, all of which can prove useful.

Remember this: even if you don't read it here, anything that works is right. Anything that helps you in your day of travail is okay.

So if you believe that sitting in the bathtub all day or sleeping in a forest will get you through your first day, *do it*.

If you do better at not smoking when you're alone, go off somewhere by yourself. If it works, it's all right.

Here are a few other ideas that you may wish to try:

- Keep busy. Keep active. And avoid those situations you used to associate with smoking.

# QUIT

- Instead of a cup of coffee after your meals, leave the table immediately and go brush your teeth.

- Go for a long walk.

- Brisk, physical activities can take your mind off smoking. This can also help work off some of the irritation you might build up when "going it alone."

- Spend as much time as you possibly can in those places where you cannot smoke. We've already mentioned the bathtub and the shower. But have you thought about going to the library, spending an afternoon in court, or going to a hospital?

- See a movie. Sightsee. Take a tour of your local fire station. Visit a mortuary. Go swimming. Go to church.

- Reread Chapter 2 of this program.

- Lay in a supply of your favorite snacks and goodies. When the urge to smoke strikes, chew gum or suck on a mint.

# QUIT

- Reread your study pages again and pay particular attention to your reasons for quitting smoking. Remind yourself of the consequences of continuing to smoke.

- Tell yourself you will not—just for ten minutes—smoke a cigarette. Then, take a long walk. Chances are, you won't feel like having that cigarette when you get back.

- Brush your teeth following every meal.

- Give up your coffee breaks just for now.

- When the urge to smoke strikes, start making telephone calls to nonsmokers who can help you on your way.

- Leave your car at home. Take a bus.

- Try walking instead of riding.

- Work off some steam. Go jogging, biking, walking, weightlifting, tennis—anything that will get your mind off of cigarettes.

- Read today's obituary column in your newspaper. Make special note of those who died at your age or younger. Ask yourself, "Was cigarette smoking responsible for this person's early demise? Could that have been me?"

There are lots of other tips you'll be able to dream up on your own. Use them often, and above all, try to keep yourself as busy as possible.

## What About The Patch?

In recent years, a variety of nicotine replacement therapies have been developed to help quitters cope with withdrawal symptoms. There's nicotine gum, sprays, patches, inhalers, and prescription drugs like Zyban.

To be effective, nicotine replacement therapy should be used in conjunction with a quitting program like this one. These remedies provide a substitute source of nicotine and can reduce or eliminate withdrawal symptoms. And when you're not suffering from withdrawal, it's easier to stay off cigarettes.

On the downside, replacement therapies are not cheap, costing anywhere from $25 to more than $50 each week, plus any prescribing doctor's fee. Moreover, not everyone can use such therapies. People with certain medical conditions and pregnant women should not use them. When using the patch, it is very important that users do not smoke cigarettes or use tobacco in any form.

The bottom line for many smokers is this: since most people quit smoking without benefit of either a formal quit-smoking program or replacement therapies, the overall benefits of these therapies might be marginal.

## The First Day Is The Hardest

This is particularly true when you remember that Day One is always the worst day. Regardless of how difficult this first day can be—they all get easier from here on in. Time is a great healer. And as time passes, the dreadful preoccupation and that awful craving disappear without drugs, without patches.

It's also interesting to note that there are a lot of smokers who really don't believe that they can get through one day without a smoke. Once you've done it, you'll be amazed at how it boosts your confidence, helps make you ready and rarin' to go for Day Two.

But don't get too cocky! Self-confidence of an overbearing and haughty nature will bring you back to smoking faster than you ever could imagine. So cool it.

And remember, take it a day at a time. Have I said that enough times? Keep busy. Keep active. It gets nothing but easier from here on in.

## Help From The Internet

The Internet has created world-wide vistas of news and self-help for the millions of Americans who are trying to kick the habit. There are literally hundreds of sites where you can buy quit-smoking products (including a few scams). But there are also some very useful websites that feature chat rooms, message boards, resources, and plenty of links to other smoking cessation addresses you might find useful.

Any of the major search engines can put you in touch with these sites. Plus I've created a starter list of sites where I've found compelling information.

### BLAIR'S QUITTING SMOKING RESOURCES
**(www.quitsmokingsupport.com)**
A nicely assembled website where you'll find plenty of information and lots of links to even more.

### FOUNDATIONS FOR INNOVATIONS IN NICOTINE DEPENDENCE
**(www.findhelp.com)**
Plenty of helpful news, articles, and publications, plus chat rooms, message boards, and other resources.

### QUITNET
**(www.quitnet.org)**
Another nicely designed site with

a full lineup of self-help tools including guides, calendars, directories, anniversary email service, and more.

### THE NO SMOKE CAFE
**(www.clever.net/chrisco/nosmoke)**
A real folksy site with chat rooms, message boards, and other information.

### TRANSFORMATIONS
**(www.transformations.com)**
Includes chat room, message boards, resources, and other information.

## Major Health Organizations Involved in Quitting Smoking

You might also wish to drop in for a visit to websites of major health organizations that can offer you additional online help and information about quitting smoking.

AMERICAN CANCER SOCIETY
**(www.cancer.org)**

AMERICAN LUNG ASSOCIATION
**(www.lungusa.org)**

NATIONAL CANCER INSTITUTE
**(www.nci.nih.gov)**

AMERICAN HEART ASSOCIATION
**(www.amhrt.org)**

OFFICE ON SMOKING AND HEALTH,
CENTERS FOR DISEASE CONTROL
AND PREVENTION
**(www.cdc.gov/nccdphp/osh/
tobacco.htm)**

You'll find lots more Internet self-help from the major portals like Yahoo!, AltaVista, and Microsoft Network. Seek out the most interesting and potentially helpful sites before your Quit Day. When your magical day arrives, you'll know just where to go for solid, *caring* help.

# 8

## Quit Day and Beyond

At about this point in a program about quitting smoking, you might expect to hear a lot of hand-holding advice while your author leads you through a day-by-day count-down until you reach some arbitrary "safe" point, such as two or three weeks.

Sorry. You'll find none of that sort of thing here.

Yes, I will give you strokes for making it to this point in your program. You've quit smoking for one or more days—that's terrific and I hope you go all the way. But the truth is, millions of smokers have made it to this point, only to chuck it all and go back to their old, death-defying, smoking behavior. In fact, the Surgeon General's Report on the Consequences of Smoking For Women reports that although some 3.5 million people give up smoking each year, many more smokers, another 12.8 million persons, tried to quit but were unsuccessful.

So rather than passing out all sorts of congratulatory messages and back-slapping praise, let's instead spend our time on your chief concern: how to continue your new nonsmoking behavior.

## When Does The Preoccupation End?

You have really given up smoking cigarettes, according to one former smoker, when you quit *thinking* about giving up cigarettes.

Perhaps this isn't too far from the truth. Giving up cigarettes is like giving up anything else: that which we try to quit suddenly assumes a new importance in our life as we become preoccupied with its absence. Whether it's sex, high-fat foods, or your coffee break, they become all the more dear when we can't have them anymore.

This preoccupation affects different smokers to different degrees. During the first few days, almost all new nonsmokers experience considerable preoccupation with cigarettes and smoking. For some, the obsession begins to wane in just a few days. Others remain preoccupied for several days, even weeks.

And for everybody—and you can corroborate this with any former smoker—the occasional craving for a smoke may remain for a lifetime.

And here's something else which is for sure: when we stop *thinking* about not smoking, it is a lot easier not to smoke.

Therefore, the best thing for you to do right now is to *keep busy*. When your mind is on something else, it cannot be smoking. It's as simple as that. It is as important as that.

## Your Weight

Some people, as you might have heard, gain weight when they quit smoking. Perhaps that's because many people substitute food for cigarettes. When they puff less, they eat more.

Many people could use the few extra pounds they might gain. For them, a couple of extra pounds are an unexpected blessing that enhances their new, nonsmoking freedom.

However, those who gain unwanted weight may wish to consider, at some later time, a weight-watching program to keep their weight within acceptable limits. I say "later" because most people have enough to worry about just giving up cigarettes, without taking on the additional burden of fretting over extra pounds.

The danger here is to overdramatize weight gains to the point where fear of extra poundage takes priority over giving up cigarettes. We've all heard that excuse: "I'd quit smoking but I'm afraid of the weight I'd gain."

The fear is unfounded. Most smokers who quit do not gain excessive weight. And those who do would have to gain a great deal of weight to equal the medical hazards that pack-a-day smoking presents. In fact, some experts say you'd have to gain up to ninety excess pounds to equal the hazards of pack-a-day smoker risks.

Moreover, if your tendency is to reach for a snack instead of a smoke, remember, you can always reach for a low-calorie snack if you feel weight may be a problem.

## Your Doctor

If in doubt, see your doctor. And by all means, get yourself a checkup—even before you set your Quit Day.

One of the niftiest things about getting a complete checkup is receiving the welcome news that you're in tip-top shape. Such a report offers hope that you haven't screwed up your body in a major way by smoking . . . that you are "starting over" in a sense, with a reasonably clean bill of health.

I say "reasonably" because it will be only after a number of years of nonsmoking that your body—heart, lungs, and other organs—will become as healthy as those of a person who has never smoked. For some, they may never return to that state of healthiness. But believe me when I say there's nothing nicer than a doctor's clean bill of health.

## One Cigarette is Too Many One Thousand Aren't Enough

Many people reach a point in their nonsmoking lives when they feel they have the situation "under control," whatever that means. And that having a cigarette, just this once, won't hurt.

Thinking like this should ring a bell in your head. You're about to lose control.

# QUIT

For while this situation is not perfectly analogous to the alcoholic and his "first drink to fall off the wagon," there is one definite similarity: neither smoker nor alcoholic ordinarily stops at just one. And for the smoker it can easily be the beginning of a short road back to steady smoking, just as before.

So please take my word for it. That first cigarette will be extremely distasteful to you. It will make you dizzy, even nauseous. But after several smokes it will be just like old times. And I'll simply say right here, the risk of "just one" simply isn't worth it.

# What To Do If
# You Do Not Succeed

In this program of giving up cigarettes, there are no failures.

There are just two kinds of people; those who do give up smoking and those who do not. Your intrinsic worth remains the same whatever the outcome.

I mention this because some people who try to give up cigarettes view their attempt and subsequent "slip" as a sign of personal weakness.

Quitting cigarettes is a process, rather than a single event or act. And just as I have tried to give you

171

the proper mental attitude about what kind of cigarette smoker you are, I also have tried to emphasize that this process takes time. If the learning does not take immediately, you must try again and again.

Why? Because quitting takes time. Just as we did not enjoy smoking the very first time we tried, we may not enjoy our new nonsmoking behavior immediately. Some studies suggest, for example, that it takes six times to quit before a person actually succeeds. Each time you try, you learn something new about yourself and your habit. In other words, the more times you try, the more likely you are to succeed.

So if you have a remission in your program, don't give up the entire plan.

## What Did You Do?

In an earlier chapter, I pointed out that many former smokers "talked themselves" into smoking again when the craving for that first cigarette struck.

I also said that perhaps they never really reached a committed decision to quit smoking in the first place. If you started smoking again,

173

I want you to go back and try to remember what was going on in your mind when you wanted to have that first cigarette.

Actually, the *content* of that conversation matters little. So whether you said to yourself, "It's too much of a hassle," or "I'll gain too much weight," is not the question. But it does matter a great deal what you did when those sentences started popping into your head.

Did you, for example, merely mull the matter over in your head instead of trying to combat that thinking with positive action?

Did you try to talk yourself out

of that cigarette at all? Did you call anyone for help? Did you go online to a chat room full of "quitters" just like you who are sharing their experiences for the common good?

Did you reread Chapter 2 of this program? Did you take a cold shower or take a long walk? Did you chew some gum or promise yourself that you wouldn't have a smoke?

The bottom line is, when the urge to smoke struck, what did you do?

If you did nothing, I suggest you go back and reevaluate your reasons for quitting.

That's really what this program is all about. I believe that if your commitment is there, you will take the action—begrudgingly or otherwise—that you believe is appropriate to avoid that first cigarette. If the commitment isn't there, you'll have trouble.

If you tried some of these suggestions and still started smoking, the process is still working. What you did was a step in the right direction, but simply was insufficient.

So try it again. Pick it up from Chapter 2 and set a new Quit Day for yourself.

Think over in your mind again what caused you to have a cigarette and how you'll handle things differently next time. And don't waste a lot of time before you launch into a new quit-smoking program. The longer you wait, the harder it becomes as start anew.

If you want to make it, you can. But you'll have to try again.

And while you're setting your new Quit Day, talk to some of your friends who have given up smoking. Many will tell you that they too did not quit smoking on their first attempt. They will probably tell you it took several tries to accomplish the task.

Look at it this way. It probably took you years and years to build this habit to where it is today. Give yourself the benefit of the doubt and realize that it may take considerable time and effort to eradicate this deadly habit.

And remember this well: if it were all that easy to quit smoking, the habit wouldn't be as bad as they say it is. I know you can do it. Try again. You *can* set yourself free. Good luck. And long life.

# Here's Why
# I Want To Quit Smoking!

- 

- 

- 

- 

-

# Here's Why
# I Want To Quit Smoking!

- 

- 

- 

- 

-

# Here's Why
# I Want To Quit Smoking!

- 
- 
- 
- 
-

# Here's Why
## I Want To Quit Smoking!

- 

- 

- 

- 

-

# Here's Why
# I Want To Quit Smoking!

- 
- 
- 
- 
-

# Here's Why
# I Want To Quit Smoking!

- 
- 
- 
- 
-

# Here's Why
# I Want To Quit Smoking!

- 
- 
- 
- 
-

# Here's Why
## I Want To Quit Smoking!

- 
- 
- 
- 
-

# Here's Why
# I Want To Quit Smoking!

- 

- 

- 

- 

-

# Here's Why
# I Want To Quit Smoking!

- 

- 

- 

- 

-

| TIME | CIGARETTE RANKING | RANK |
|------|-------------------|------|
|      |                   |      |
|      |                   |      |
|      |                   |      |
|      |                   |      |
|      |                   |      |

## CIGARETTE RANKING

| TIME | | | | | | | RANK |
|------|---|---|---|---|---|---|------|
| | | | | | | | |
| | | | | | | | |
| | | | | | | | |
| | | | | | | | |
| | | | | | | | |
| | | | | | | | |
| | | | | | | | |

| TIME | CIGARETTE RANKING | RANK |
|------|-------------------|------|
|      |                   |      |
|      |                   |      |
|      |                   |      |
|      |                   |      |
|      |                   |      |
|      |                   |      |
|      |                   |      |
|      |                   |      |

| CIGARETTE RANKING | | | | | | | | | |
|---|---|---|---|---|---|---|---|---|---|
| TIME | RANK | | | | | | | | |
| | | | | | | | | | |

| TIME | CIGARETTE RANKING | RANK |
|------|-------------------|------|
|      |                   |      |
|      |                   |      |
|      |                   |      |
|      |                   |      |
|      |                   |      |
|      |                   |      |
|      |                   |      |
|      |                   |      |

| CIGARETTE RANKING | | | | | | | | |
|---|---|---|---|---|---|---|---|---|
| TIME | RANK | | | | | | | |
| | | | | | | | | |

| TIME | CIGARETTE RANKING | RANK |
|------|-------------------|------|
|      |                   |      |
|      |                   |      |
|      |                   |      |
|      |                   |      |
|      |                   |      |

| CIGARETTE RANKING | | |
|---|---|---|
| TIME | | RANK |
| | | |
| | | |
| | | |
| | | |
| | | |
| | | |
| | | |
| | | |

| TIME | CIGARETTE RANKING | RANK |
|------|-------------------|------|
|      |                   |      |
|      |                   |      |
|      |                   |      |
|      |                   |      |
|      |                   |      |
|      |                   |      |
|      |                   |      |
|      |                   |      |

| TIME | CIGARETTE RANKING | | | | | | | | RANK |
|------|-------------------|--|--|--|--|--|--|--|------|
|      |                   |  |  |  |  |  |  |  |      |
|      |                   |  |  |  |  |  |  |  |      |
|      |                   |  |  |  |  |  |  |  |      |
|      |                   |  |  |  |  |  |  |  |      |
|      |                   |  |  |  |  |  |  |  |      |
|      |                   |  |  |  |  |  |  |  |      |
|      |                   |  |  |  |  |  |  |  |      |

| TIME | CIGARETTE RANKING | RANK |
| --- | --- | --- |
| | | |
| | | |
| | | |
| | | |
| | | |
| | | |

## CIGARETTE RANKING

| TIME | | | | | | | | RANK |
|------|---|---|---|---|---|---|---|------|
| | | | | | | | | |
| | | | | | | | | |
| | | | | | | | | |
| | | | | | | | | |
| | | | | | | | | |
| | | | | | | | | |
| | | | | | | | | |

| TIME | CIGARETTE RANKING | RANK |
|------|-------------------|------|
|      |                   |      |
|      |                   |      |
|      |                   |      |
|      |                   |      |
|      |                   |      |
|      |                   |      |
|      |                   |      |
|      |                   |      |

| CIGARETTE RANKING | |
| --- | --- |
| TIME | RANK |
| | |
| | |
| | |
| | |
| | |
| | |
| | |
| | |

| TIME | CIGARETTE RANKING | RANK |
| --- | --- | --- |
| | | |
| | | |
| | | |
| | | |
| | | |
| | | |

# Notes

# Notes

# **Notes**

# <u>Notes</u>